*[Handwritten inscription:]*

Carolyn,
May the words
round the pages of
this book bless you
the way the experience
performed me. Thank
for your support!
Love
[signature]

# Own Your Power
## The Keys To A Conscious Awakening

Dr. Maria Barnes, N.D.

Copyright © 2012 Maria Barnes

ISBN:1542629489
ISBN-13:9781542629485

# DEDICATION

Due to the love of my family and friends this book was possible. I dedicate this first of many books to my family, Madison Grant, Carrington Grant, Cedric Pendleton, and to my younger soul sister, Nandi Tibbett. You keep me motivated because I know you are watching and I feel your genuine love. You also give me hope and have been by my side throughout some of my happiest and hardest moments..

# CONTENTS

# ACKNOWLEDGMENTS

I  want to thank my parents, Calvin and Gloria Barnes, for loving me unconditionally and giving me exactly what I needed to become the person I am today: LOVE.
I would also like to acknowledge Scott Benton who encouraged me to write, the stranger I met at the Goat Farm coffee shop who so unselfishly helped me refine my book design. Becky Greiner who edited my work, Sonya Lloyd who took a moment to hold me accountable, and everyone who I may not have mentioned by name but you encouraged me to get to the finish line.

# 1 BACKGROUND

This book is written not only about my journey, but also about how to help you through your own journey towards love, health, and happiness that will also lead you to owning a power we all have possessed from the time we entered a realm of human living. Going through life, I wish I would have had someone to guide me through finding myself and achieving balance in my life, and that's why I am here to teach you.

Among other things, I will teach you the importance of leaving worry in the next room and removing all negative thoughts, allowing love to stay in the driver's seat. Love is the key to happiness and wealth. It bears repeating:

# "Love is the key to happiness and wealth"

Love is the secret to altering the vibrational frequencies of all things you desire in this lifetime. I came from a very loving family but did not have wealth, and although they believed in God and love with everything they have, they did not trust their ability to produce more in their lives. Not because they did not want it, but because, like most, they did not learn what it means to live every aspect of their lives with consciousness and control their mental capabilities in order to harness and attract improvement and a better way of life.

My words are not just about healing; they are about the motivation and support that we all need when we are alone and doubt begins to set in. When you begin to wonder, "Am I capable and do I deserve the reality of such big dreams?" I am here to tell you: Yes, you do!

As a child, I was always a dreamer of doing big things. I can recall admiring the big houses that other people lived in and the fancy clothes they adorned themselves in. Ever since then, I felt like I was destined to do something big, and that I would one day use that as a way to help provide my family with the things they denied themselves from thinking they could have.

I did not grow up with a lot of material possessions, but I did grow up within a family who surrounded me with love and helped me believe in myself. I was a difficult child; I wanted to do things my way, thought I knew it all, and wanted so desperately to be "grown" before my time. My mother was very instrumental in the strength I have today. She came from a family of strong-willed people, however. They had secrets that they held onto, which prevented many of them from living out their full potential. I have learned not only from my own experiences but also from the lives of my family to not accept NO for an answer, and that there is always a way through.

I am the youngest of three with a brother, Garland, and my sister, Caprice. We had a great childhood together; so much laughter and glorious time spent together. My parents, Calvin and Gloria, were born and raised in Akron, Ohio. They both came from relatively large families. My mother was raised along with 11 other siblings, and my dad, well, his history is one that I still haven't quite grasped.

What I do know is that my father grew up with eight siblings, although his parents both died while he was young and he was raised by my mother's aunt. I have aunts and uncles that are really cousins by blood, typical within black families and among the things you don't know until everyone gets old enough to start dropping and understanding family secrets. I come from a proud family on both sides, a lineage of many college graduates and others who obtained professional trades.

My father worked for Firestone, a driving force for many families in Akron, but he and my mother were also hair stylists and owned a salon. Life to me felt pretty good at that time. Then, one day, Firestone shut down, and it felt like the rest of the city did as well. My father started having visions at that time, which brings us to the move. It was time to leave Akron; my dad wanted to experience more from the hair business, so we picked up and landed ourselves in Atlanta, Georgia.

I remember arriving in Atlanta very vividly; the buildings looked so tall and the city felt like it swallowed us up. My mother broke down in tears and, although she confidently followed my dad, still questioned whether they were doing the right thing. Life changed very abruptly and survival mode kicked in for my family. We went from being surrounded by family and friends to being surrounded by the faces of strangers, wondering who to trust. My parents got lost in the need to provide for us, and as the years began rolling by, I watched my father drift farther and farther away from his original plan.

I witnessed the contradiction between his desire to make the leap and my mother's concern about the landing. I watched them struggle, and as I witnessed from the outside, little did I know that I would subsequently inherit their subconscious vibrational frequency of lack and of not having enough.

I wanted more for my parents and decided that when I grew up, I was going to be responsible for giving them a better material life. When we moved to Atlanta, I was an over achieving student. I was at the top of my class, loved to read, and was very outgoing. Somewhere along the way, in the midst of surviving, I lost the appetite to be the best student. I got lost in the peer pressure of being cool and accepted, which distracted me from making good grades.

I did enough at school to get by, and that is exactly what life began giving me in return: enough to get me by. Being the youngest of three, I had to make sure I was not left behind; I needed to not only keep up, but stand out. That has been the pattern for me into my adulthood; don't just keep up; stand out. I always felt the need to do something great, something bigger than average, and writing this book with a big story to tell has definitely made that list. I remember being told by a white teacher who, in my opinion, never embraced black students, that I could not write. She used to mark my papers up with red ink, leaving me with very little confidence and lack of desire to write because she never told me how I could become better, only that I couldn't do it. Another reason that I'm writing to you now is to tell you that, in case you have also been told, "you can't" by someone who is only interested in holding back your potential - yes, you can!

As a result of my own experience, I went through a number of years believing that I could not write very well. Well, here I am, yet another stigma I have broken through. Today I stand with great confidence and powerful positive energy, and I attribute my growing pains to where I am today as well as that desire I developed as a little girl to rise above the crowd.

Today we are exactly what we have invested in ourselves from our past; choices that we made that led us down various roads. The beauty in life is at any given moment you have the ability to change lanes, change the road you're on, and even change your route. You are powerful. I felt power as a child, but I did not really have the right guidance to show me how to use my power for good. I am not referring to the kind of good that is kindness to others or of having respect for other people; I am referring to the kind of power that can create individual well-being, the lifestyle I always admired that others had from having money, the kind of power that gives you control over your life.

When I became a young adult, I did not know how to manage money and what building wealth really required, but the power that I was given and that was instilled in me was the power in taking care of my health and knowing how important it was to be active and eat healthy. The reason why you are reading this book today is because I had to fight for my life in order to change my own route. I battled two of the hardest situations of my life, then woke up and realized I was doing things all wrong. I knew I had to change my mental thinking and I had to change the money in my bank account.

In this book, I will share with you intimate details about some of my most painful experiences and how they helped me to reprogram my attitude. As you read my story, you will gain the inspiration and tools necessary to break through anything that is holding you back from rising above the crowd. I will provide you with the hope and belief through nutritional, spiritual, and mental wellness remedies because these remedies are what saved my life, and I am confident that if you apply these practices, they are powerful enough to save yours, too.

Opportunity is merely belief and preparation connecting with universal timing. Whatever you want to achieve in life, whether it's to make more money, overcome sickness or heal relationships with people, you can obtain all of those things by tapping into the power that resides inside of you. I am not more special than you and no one else is either. You and I are both winners; the only difference between those who win and those who don't is the belief that he or she can. The power is waiting to be unleashed by you, and once you decide you are ready to stop looking outside of yourself for answers when they have always existed from within, you will find the ability to not only command the things you want in life to come to you, but also accomplish all the things your imagination desires and travel the path your heart leads you. This book is about the struggles that became my ladder. It is about my need to find my true self and the surprising way life forced me to do it. I once walked through life as a victim of never having enough, harboring envy for the accomplishments that others made, thinking "why can't that be me?" I knew deep down I could get control of my life, but I was afraid I could not overcome the obstacles.

The obstacles are always the toxic people or things that we must find a way to let go of. The obstacles are typically what prevent us from moving forward; they appear too big to compete against. On the contrary, the obstacles are based on fear, and our imaginations turn them into larger obstacles. The mind is so powerful, it will make or break your life. I spent many years battling obstacles until I decided I had enough. Once I decided I'd had enough running, I turned around and saw myself. I saw that the obstacles I turned into mountains were actually small pebbles. Now that you have started this book, I want you to read it until the end because completing it will be the first step in your life to signify you are no longer going to allow fear to control you and to make decisions for your life. You will walk from a place of love, and it will give you the ability to look at that obstacle in your way and recognize it for what it is - a small pebble, and once you can kick it aside, you can obtain all things through combining logic and love.

My battle to overcome the pain left from divorce and cancer is what saved my life. I had two choices; I could have chosen to run and leave my daughter and son to live their lives without learning everything I had to teach them, or I had to turn around and fight through the mistakes I made as a young person, a failed marriage that I also contributed to, and business decisions that were causing me to live a life always wanting what someone else had. I mustered up the courage, and I chose to fight.

The scary part about making corrections in life is because it is like peeling an onion; every time you peel off one layer, there are several more layers left. I know how challenging it is to change the routines in life that have become habits, but those challenges are your programmed subconscious thoughts and beliefs. The moment you begin working towards doing something different, something better for yourself, your ego begins getting angry and tries to take back the control. Yes, I know all too well, because I had to go back to my childhood and begin reprogramming the things I heard and the lifestyle I was exposed to growing up; the challenges about money and the religious beliefs that were only creating more challenges in my life.

As you continue to read, I will share with you more detail about these experiences and how they impacted my life, what I did to overcome them, and why I emphasize the importance of controlling your health and your wealth. I am confident you will connect with me on so many levels during this journey together, and I am trusting that if you have found my book and are connecting with my words, that it is time for your breakthrough, It is time for you to catch up and rise above. It is time for you to redefine what success really is through your physical and mental well-being. It is time for you to "take back your life."

## "Take Back Your Life"

If you find yourself lost in my words, then this message is for you.

## 2 TODAY

Every morning in which the good Lord allows me to wake up, I bless my head through a Yoruba ritual, which metaphorically places a protective armor over the most powerful part of the human body.

I meditate for 20 minutes, breathing in good, positive energy and releasing the negative heavy weight of anything that should not be on my mind or in my spirit.

I offer a prayer of thanksgiving and conclude each meditation session with a brief inspirational reading.

I incorporated some of this from a powerful book by Iyanla Vasant, "Tapping the Power Within."

These four steps I take every morning, that I call emotional alkalinity, may seem like something small and insignificant, but they have become a powerful, peaceful, and necessary part of my daily routine.

## "Emotional Alkalinity"

These steps allow me to put things into perspective, connect with God and myself, and call the proper energy into my spirit.

I vividly recall the time in my life when I endured a volatile divorce and experienced financial hardship. I had to remain strong for my two young children who needed me emotionally as well as physically. Stress and worry were the two big factors in my life for eight years.

I was disappointed in myself for being in this place. I had never expected to be here and viewed it as unacceptable. I was hurt by the human behavior that takes center stage during a nasty divorce. I felt as though my life was crumbling before my very eyes. I felt powerless and robbed of my joy.

Although I felt alone in my own space, over time, I learned that my experience was merely a pebble among stones. Through much study and research, I found that many people are carrying stress on a consistent basis and that this stress is leading to a variety of negative health issues. I learned that many, like me, are consequently developing breast cancer. We are allowing stress to compromise our bodies and our quality of life.

# "EAT stands for Emotional Alkalinity Therapy"

It is a unique therapy I developed to bring balance to the mind. EAT is based on the knowledge that unresolved emotional trauma and life patterns lead to imbalances in our lives, eventually causing anything from troubled relationships to major disease.

It works by tapping into the unforeseen emotional shocks and traumas that you experience, which create a malfunction in your nervous system. These events or life patterns simultaneously become an imprint of brain, tissues, and psyche. These thoughts of information are buried in your subconscious mind and soon lead to negatively impacting the way you perceive and navigate your life.

Your body function also changes, which will create imbalances and disease. EAT works to resolve these at the source, resolving emotional shock, traumatic events, and damaging life patterns. By changing subconscious patterns and healing emotional wounds, relationships transform, hope is restored, and symptoms of illness can vanish.

I have witnessed the healing of abandonment, abuse, emotional deprivation, failure, loss, mistrust, social exclusion, dependence and more when my patients began to EAT.

The importance of taking care of your health and what you eat emotionally, physically, and mentally can determine your path in this lifetime. No matter what you want out of life, you must pay attention to what you EAT.

No one could ever understand how it feels to fight cancer unless they have had to actually walk that journey for themselves. While trying to digest the idea that life is going to become different after your receive the news, you are also told to keep stress and anxiety down, and get proper rest. But, to the contrary, stress and anxiety rise, and sleepless nights are countless. You worry about the future and are suddenly at a place in your life where you have to make serious choices about your health.

I know all too well because I was once in those shoes, trying to make choices without the influence of others and under the pressure of a health care system that even today I can't embrace. For so many years, I worked on taking care of my health and was very proud of my appearance. When I looked at myself, I saw something beautiful. The year that things really became physically hard on me, I was undergoing chemotherapy and could no longer see what I thought was beautiful not so long ago.

My energy changed, according to the people in my life, including my own inner thoughts; I thought this was clearly supposed to be the fate of my former spouse, not me. The question that runs through so many minds when attempting to swallow this news is, "why is this happening to me?" I was embarking on the path to forgiveness, and although I was still under the influence of an evil force still trying to break me, I believed I was being the better person.

I did not understand how much of my subconscious thoughts were consumed by the negative. I remember looking in the mirror, wondering who am I and asking myself the question, "is this all I have left to do?" What kind of life is this to be 43 years old with nothing behind me that I contributed to this earth to be excited over.

Yes, two beautiful children to may seem like enough, but that was never enough for me; I had bigger plans and had envisioned a much bigger purpose since childhood, but I underestimated what it would take to get me there. It was time to take a deep swallow and a big deep breath, because life was about to take me on a journey I could have never imagined; a journey of letting go, embracing truth, and learning how to command wealth, health, healing, love, and success through the power of meditation and mental control.

Health

Being healthy is not something you should have to earn; it is yours by divine right. It is your home that can be made out of hay, sticks or bricks. Both mental and physical health are often overlooked when goals are made, and not a lot of people consider maintaining or obtaining good health when brainstorming ways to improve their lives. Most talk about making more money, getting a better job, traveling more, or even finding a mate before health is even put on the front burner.

I am here to put more emphasis on the importance of having good health. I grew up listening to a bedtime story about the three little pigs; do you remember that one? The eldest pig left home and built a house made out of brick; another left and built his house out of wood, and finally the last pig set off from his mother's home and decided he was the smartest by saving resources and building his home out of hay.

While these three little pigs were growing up in their mother's home, she always told them to look out for the Big Bad Wolf. The Big Bad Wolf represents life, and the homes that were built are foundation, love, health, and wealth. If you decide to build a weak body and mind off of eating foods, drinking beverages, and failing to strengthen your faith, your poor habits are only going to compromise your foundation, and when the Big Bad Wolf comes around, all it will take is a huff and a puff and to blow your house down.

The same goes for wealth and love. How are you building your foundation: out of sticks, bricks or hay? Building something strong may take more time and money, but in the end, you will find that it was the right thing to do. I did not build a strong foundation. I made it out of high school, but I was unprepared. School did not equip me with the necessary tools in life that would help me succeed.

My parents, I believe, did the best they could, but sending me out into the world with the right skill set for life was not their focus. Their focus was on providing three kids with what they needed in order to survive at that time and experience peace within the home. I lacked a healthy relationship with money, I thought I knew about relationships with men, and I definitely did not know what I wanted to be when I grew up. If it sounds like I had no clue how to adapt to the world, you're absolutely right! I had one thing going for me, however; I found a passion in maintaining good health, which would end up saving me later on.

I invested everything I had into being the best athlete and creating the strongest and best looking body, even though I was just getting started. Interestingly enough, when you think you don't know where to start in life, you just need to start where you heart tells you to. For many of us, as soon as we decide we want to go and do something, we get stuck because we think the wall is too big to climb. But in actuality, the things we create within our minds are even bigger obstacles that don't actually exist.

With this mindset, you become your greatest enemy, and although you may want to blame your defeat on others, the only one standing in your way is yourself. People don't have power to decide your destiny or how your life is supposed to turn out; only you can decide. My health was the one area in my life I had always felt like I had control over. It became my safe place because I knew what I was doing and I knew what to expect when I did it. It wasn't until after I was married and had my first child, a girl named Madison, that I decided it was time to take my fitness journey to another level. It was time to become serious about my diet.

# "The Only One Standing In Your Way Is Yourself"

I began studying the science behind food and how it could develop the human body into anything. When I began learning about food, I started to fully realize the power I actually had and the control that I could command over my life. I felt good and confident, although many things were still missing. I could have never guessed that what that I found passion in as a child would become a large part of who I am and what makes me the person I am today.

My contribution to the world is all about health and emotional and mental well-being. Through my lifelong journey optimizing my health, I have learned how to develop a better relationship with money, and I have learned how to maintain emotional intelligence over behaviors and situations that I don't have full control over. My health challenged me to fight my way out of toxic thinking and behaviors so that I could discover how rewarding being vulnerable can truly become. Without good health, you do not stand in full control of your life, you do not stand in a place that allows you to build on a strong foundation or leave a good legacy for generations to come behind you. So I ask you this question: which is most important, health or wealth?

The answer, and I will tell you this with absolute conviction, is both. Good health is beautiful, especially when you are wealthy, and being wealthy is beneficial when you are in good health.

Spiritual Balance

When it comes to your personal relationship with food, you typically eat the same way you grew up eating unless you begin to question your own habits. Our childhood habits don't necessarily hold stock after we grow up from being under the guidance and influence of our parents and elders.

Spirituality is no different, and you more than likely left home using some of the same beliefs that were inherited from others until you began to question them for yourself. It is important for us to ask questions about religion and spirituality and challenge some of the rules that interfere with finding peace in our lives rather than focusing on not living up to how others told us we are supposed to live.

This is not religion I am referring to; religion gets in the way of the difference between love and fear. I am talking about spirituality; the energy force that connects us all together, that creates the power within us to overcome lessons and obstacles and experience growth. We are not capable of experiencing true freedom and happiness without spiritual balance. By spiritual balance, I'm talking about taking the time necessary to sit still with the power inside of you.

It is the distinction between love and fear and the strength in all of us that can make a major difference in how we move through this lifetime. I mentioned earlier there are two things needed in order to obtain full control of your life: good health and wealth. But what ties everything together, the thread that flows through it and harmonizes everything is your spiritual relationship. As you may have noticed, I did not mention with whom you should identify your spiritual balance. Why? Because it really doesn't matter; the energy is Love or Fear.

## "The Energy is Love or Fear"

You nurture one of two ways: by investing time into and understanding how to become powerful through having love behind your actions, or by F.E.A.R. - Fostering Experiences As Reality. I will discuss these in greater detail throughout this journey together. For now, it is time to begin asking yourself important questions about your personal belief system like, "Why do I attend this church when all I do is sit and daydream while I am there?" or "Will God really be mad at me because I love the same sex?" Does a power that is associated with Love really respond out of anger or F.E.A.R.? I want you to begin adopting these into your thought process NOW if you are interested in experiencing a breakthrough in your life.

If you want to remedy being stuck because you lack courage and are living your life from a place of F.E.A.R, you must be willing to challenge your present way of thinking. Your experiences have shaped you into the person you are today; if the only memories you have from them are negative, you must be ready to revisit them in order to find the love that existed during the time when you made those decisions. Rediscover the love that was combined with your intent when you went into the relationship, even though it may have ended badly.

Relationships that become bad are not there to make your life miserable; they show up because there is a force of energy that no longer requires a connection. That lost connection may be forever or for just a short while, but the point is that the other person is vibrating at a higher level than you are, and not everyone can move through their spiritual journey simultaneously.

We came into this world alone, which means we will have to sometimes leave other people as we move through it. If we cannot make those decisions consciously on our own, our subconscious mind has a way in asking the Universe to move them for us.

## F.E.A.R.

Fear is the biggest and most dangerous monster that will prevent many people from achieving their real purpose in life. It is the invisible monster who grabs you by your mind and convinces you that whatever seems too big or too scary, don't do it and stay right where you are so you can protect yourself from the possibility of failure, the chance you may fall on your face when trying something new and exciting.

Well, this thing called fear, that big, scary invisible monster means Fostering Experiences As Reality! It means you are collecting things you go through in life and stripping away all positive lessons, only holding on to the negative and the reluctance to try again. We allow fear to keep us stuck because we stay hung up on our past, allowing our past to become our reality and our present.

When we have the wrong people surrounding us, we allow them to feed us their F.E.A.R. You may have a spouse who does not know how to understand failure as part of the formula for success; therefore, they feed you F.E.AR.

We are at a constant battle to move beyond our fears, and many aren't strong enough to make it to the other side. You have to learn to look at life in order to understand that, although we make our own bed and it may not always be a comfortable one, karmic law is in place to use the challenges we face to help us grow.

When growth happens, the only job you have is to make a choice. You can choose to overcome by trying to land that dream job even though you have been turned down three times; you can go and audition for that part even if it has been given to someone else twice; you can start a new business and take what you learned from the failure of the last two. There are so many valuable lessons we must take from our past experiences, it is a misuse of energy to assume that something bad will happen every time you try.

You have to move beyond your fears and trust that you have a divine right to WIN! Your F.E.A.R.s are not reality, they are not your present. Your F.E.A.R.s do not have the right to control your life and you must move towards releasing them in order for them to reside where they belong - in your past.

We will talk more about how you can release those fears, and I will also share with you many of the F.E.A.Rs I had to overcome, including the one that kept me from writing this book for a long time. Remember that you are a winner, and that you deserve a breakthrough, but in order to achieve it, you must be willing to experience challenging lessons to help get you there.

# "F.E.A.R – Fostering Experiences As Reality"

<u>Emotional Intelligence</u>

For the last several years, researchers have been particularly interested in a certain region of the brain responsible for emotions and feelings. A researcher by the name of Paul Ekman identified that we have six universal facial expressions: anger, happiness, sadness, surprise, disgust and fear.

He believed that through the activation of particular muscles, these expressions could be emphasized on the face. Additionally, he found that various brain regions are responsible for the feelings behind these expressions, and we will focus on the two that are the most toxic and disruptive in our lives: fear and anger.

I began with some background information about emotional intelligence because we must first talk about this concept before highlighting fear and anger. Have you ever had an argument and allowed your anger to take you to a place that you would later regret? This probably occurred hours after your heart rate came down and you were no longer fueled by rage.

How many times can you recall "flying off the cuff" without really taking a step back to consider the consequences of your actions because you were caught up in the moment? Too often, we find ourselves going nowhere in life because we lack emotional intelligence; the ability to allow our emotions to pass through us without putting negative energy into our reactions.

Lack of emotional intelligence tears relationships apart, creates failures in business, and causes us to lose more than what we started with. Emotional intelligence is a key part of our mental fitness, and if you don't have a handle on your emotions, you can't take control of your life. And when I talk about taking control, I am not referring to pretending that problems don't exist out of fear that you won't be able to control your emotions. No, I mean seeing a problem, looking at it head-on, intelligently weighing all of the options, and choosing the most sensible one. If you don't understand how to control your emotions you are not ready be in control of power. When you vote for President of the USA you would look for someone who you believe could be hold such a powerful position in office by making good decisions for the country without leading decisions by random emotions. Emotional intelligence is exactly the same skill set you should learn how to possess in order to maintain some level of control over your life.

Consider every time you get angry over something in life, your body requires more energy to manage either one of those emotions. This means that whatever you may need to properly digest food, rest well at night, or create new ideas you can't operate at a productive capacity because the energy necessary to function is allocated towards the chemical released from the anger emotion. Every step you take to move forward you take a half step back just from the ignorance in recognizing the only person losing in maintaining anger is you.

Making good choices for any problem or situation that requires an answer will allow you to sleep at night without your conscious telling you that you made the wrong choice; the decision that will allow you to continue moving forward in a positive way as you take back control of your life. It is difficult to make good decisions while also overlooking negative circumstances that cause you to feel as though you are "throwing in the towel" or accepting loss.

You are not losing when you make the right decisions for your emotional well-being; you are

WINNING and winners don't always see their wins until later. Sometimes winners must feel that the right decision has been made before they feel victory. I recall my divorce vividly and the challenges I struggled to overcome internally because I was allowing negativity to control me. I felt beat up and drained from those experiences at the hands of people who were actually miserable within themselves.

During this trying time, I had to overcome attaching myself to negative emotions, although I felt like the answer to achieving that was to lose and allow those negative people to walk over and defeat me. The right thing to do was to respond with love, because sometimes you have to lose to win. The more love I gave to myself by reinforcing who I was and what I deserved in this life, the more negativity moved further away from me. Soon, the negativity moved far enough away that I could breathe and begin focusing on getting my life back in order. Choosing to do the right thing, even in the midst of wanting to respond to a more harmful and toxic emotion, was maturing. I was learning how to maintain emotional intelligence.

## Wealth

Money, for those who don't have it, is often viewed as being evil, even though they do actually want it. Money is a necessary resource just like exercise, healthy food, and meditation. Money represents accessing your ability to live a full life. How can one say that one wants to live his or her best life but doesn't have the resources to travel the world and become immersed in the ways of others? How can you live a full life without being able to afford the opportunities that give you the experiences of fulfillment?

Money is necessary, and you are no different than those who have it and those who are working towards having it. You are as deserving of it as any person in a crowded room; you just have to know it is your divine right, and once you know it, you have to be willing to do what is necessary to earn it. Without this valuable lesson, I would not be able to write this chapter.

You see, I had to figure out my relationship with money; I had to learn how to attract money in order to build wealth. My first task was to acknowledge that I wanted to earn money and to begin respecting those who had obtained it in their lifetime. Money is not evil nor is it bad, it is those who are vibrating low negative energy who do bad things with it or for it. Just like marriage; it is not marriage that creates bad things, it is the two people who define how it behaves.

What having money looks like or how it is used has nothing to do with money itself; it has everything to do with the person in charge of its employment. If you look hard enough, you will find many people doing great things in the world who have it. It is only when you believe that you are inadequate at making money that you only see the negative stories associated to it. As a young girl, I remember witnessing my mother and father interacting over an idea my father developed.

I would get very excited for him, and I could feel his desire to want to make something more of his life and for his family, but on the flip side, I got the sense that my mother wasn't so confident about the outcome. Although she would eventually give him her verbal support, she was afraid to want more in her life for the fear of never getting it. I was at odds with my mother over witnessing this experience and the fleeting energy that my father had after coming to her with excitement.

I felt I needed to carry that torch for my father and finish something I knew he was trying to accomplish, but I had to get over layers of hurdles in my own life first. One of them was removing the F.E.A.R of failure. Witnessing my parents attempt to do better without experiencing success left an imprint in my subconscious mind that success just wasn't possible, even though I was still determined to try. I had to work very hard to leave that little girl behind with the confidence that she had an awesome childhood that included laughter, love, and happiness.

I had to leave her behind in order to focus solely on my present, which, in reality, is also my future. Today, I am a woman who can tell you with confidence that I love making money and having the option to use it for the greater good of my family and for others who may be in need of my help. YOU too can remove negative stigmas that are holding you back from the flow of abundance.

YOU can peel away the layers in your mental attitude so you can build wealth and set yourself free from the anxiety and worry that are coupled with lack of financial resources.

I realize this book is not about how to make money, so we won't venture too far into the how, but because it is about controlling power you already posess, you need to understand the importance in getting healthy, developing spiritual and emotional balance, and making enough money to live your life exactly the way you choose.

## "Peel Away The Layers In Your Mental Attitude to Build Wealth and Set Yourself Free"

## 3 THE JOURNEY

Let's begin with how I even came to a place of standing so strong. I shared with you a little about my childhood and how those experiences helped shape who I became, but now let's fast forward to when life first became a bigger challenge for me as a grown woman. In fact, life threw me multiple curve balls.

Part of my journey is about looking at the larger picture; at everything that became difficult for me to handle, and I had to use those curve balls to find the light within the darkness. I had to learn how to take everything that could have driven me to suicide, depression, eating disorders, and death from poor health, and to find love within myself.

I fought myself for a number of years, blaming my decisions on circumstances and blaming my family for passing hard times onto me. I only viewed others who were doing better than me as my enemies because I was jealous that my life was falling apart, and I wanted someone else to take my pain. In order for you to understand my journey, I will share with you the deepest parts of my history: my marriage, divorce, cancer, and some of my family history.

Yes, my lemons became, for me, my lemonade. They taught me the most valuable lessons about myself, and when I decided to stop looking so hard at others and take a look at my own back yard, well, let's just say it was like trying to find my way through a dark forest. I believe that by me sharing my journey with you, this will help you maintain the momentum or gain the courage to go to your own back yard, survey the bigger picture, and take a look at everything that needs to be cleaned out.

We all have old dead plants and weeds that need to be pulled up and removed in order to emphasize the beauty in life. We all get caught up in judging the work that others are doing sometimes, not knowing what all that person had to go through to get there. Climbing to the top requires work, and most of the work involves personal growth and shaking loose the baggage that no longer belong in our backyards.

When you wake up in the morning, without thinking you go through your routine in order to get ready for your day. You may make your bed, brush your teeth and wash your face, shower, groom your hair, get dressed, possibly prepare breakfast, and head out the door. If you decided that something within that routine needed to change because it was causing you to be late every morning, you would change it or change the time you get up in the morning. The same goes for the habits or way of thinking that are preventing you from accomplishing the things you want out of life. If you want to achieve starting your own business, you must make room in your life to focus on the needs of the business, and it can't be done if you have too many things that disrupt your ability to achieve success. You must be willing to go deep into the walls of your own life, whether you are looking at your past, or considering how you are making decisions today, in order to create the life you truly want. Clean out your own backyard.

Marriage

An interesting word and ongoing topic that opens the floor to many mixed views and opinions. The millennials look at the concept of marriage and hold up a cross as if it is the same as holding a conversation with a vampire or some other mythical creature of which they must be wary. They choose to live life longer without the extra responsibility of answering to someone else.

The mental way of processing a happy and free lifestyle is now more realistic alone when before it could only truly be envisioned with another person. When thinking about marriage, life is very different now, although marriage is still part of the traditional way of life. I was married at age 28, and honestly, I love what marriage did for me. It taught me how much more two could accomplish when on the same wave of thinking. It taught me about the importance of men and what strengths they bring to the table that women may not always have. It also taught me the importance of teamwork. I wasn't ready for marriage nor marriage and children, but that is exactly the way my story went.

I was married and within the same year I became pregnant with my first child, and from there, a different Maria enters the stage. I have coached many couples and listened to many stories, including revisiting my own, to understand that marriage typically becomes the hardest between thirty and forty years of age. In your thirties is when you start realizing that whoever you thought you were, you are not that person, and that many of those who you considered friends begin to not appear as genuine.

The decisions you have made are now creating sadness within you that can be misconstrued as a mistake. Life has become very different at this time, and you even begin looking at your spouse and wondering, "Who is this person and can I make it in this marriage?" That was clearly my story. Everything about my life felt wrong except for my two children. The man I first married and I were both brought up very differently. I was a freethinker and spoke my mind even when it got me in trouble, and I watched my father work as hard as he could to make it as an entrepreneur.

I believed in the freedom that comes with working for yourself. As a child, I was always thinking of ways to start a business and make money. I wasn't very good at the money aspect once I got it, because I wasn't used to having it. Spending, for me, was like a burning bush in my pocket. My former husband grew up very differently. His parents came from another country, worked hard, and built something from nothing within their jobs that they occupied for many years and eventually retired from. They saved wisely, and always made very conservative decisions throughout their lives.

I was far from conservative. I took risks that were not all good at the time, and that is really the dagger that drove my marriage towards divorce. Some people think marriage is hard, but divorce, in my opinion, is even harder. It takes more energy to be negative than it does to be positive. In other words, love flows freely and effortlessly, but hate and anger are forces that require work and rob your body of what is needed in order to keep your other physiological systems working properly.

My marriage was no mistake; it was a part of a growing process for not only me, but also for a man who thankfully today, I can call my friend. However how we got there is more than a chapter out of a book.

## WHO ARE YOU?

Have you ever looked in the mirror or laid awake at night wondering what is really going on in your life and what does it all mean? These questions started surfacing in my thirties. At some point, you begin to realize that everything you thought you had figured out about your life and what you wanted to do with it is not real. Everything has now changed due to things you may have experienced or even just because the world is beginning to look different to you now. That is when anxiety begins to set in and you begin to think, "Oh my God, I am so old and I have wasted so many years; If I change everything around it will only set me back!"

You begin panicking, because now you are looking at a sign that tells you to DETOUR and take another path. When you are uncertain about arriving at the right destination, the world around you becomes very scary.

I was in that same car, traveling down that same road, reaching the DETOUR sign. I was slipping away from myself; I didn't even look like myself anymore. At that time, I was working in a corporate position as a financial analyst, sitting in a cubicle surrounded by people who carried the energy of puppets being controlled by stagehands. The energy in Corporate America, no matter what company I jumped into, was simply not part of my genetic make up.

I was born to create, move around, inspire, and be free. I felt it all the way down to my bones, but when I got excited about that feeling, I would be brought down again from being in a marriage that pulled me to stay in line, follow the rules, and take low risks. I wanted more for my life, and one day I was visited by an older version of me, and I did not like the way I looked. I had the appearance of wear and tear, and I knew I had to make some hard decisions; I had to leave my marriage in order to set myself free. With two small children and no plan, I walked away. I took a risk because I wanted more out of life. I am not suggesting you walk away from your marriage in order to create change, but for me at that time, it was my only way.

The story about my marriage is for you to understand that, in life, there are situations that are holding you back; that are simply not good for you in that moment. You must be willing to sacrifice what is necessary in order to move forward, and that may mean accepting consequences that will make life hard for you before you see the light at the end of the tunnel. I regret leaving my marriage the way that I did, but I had no other solution at that time. I just knew how to run, and so I did. Sometimes, if running is the only way to get away when you are emotionally tied to something or someone, you must run.

## DIVORCE

Writing about this part of my life is interesting for me, because this was the catalyst for my cancer diagnosis. My divorce was hard on me; maybe because I did not want to be at odds with someone. I did not want someone I still loved to be angry with me for a decision I made, and although I felt was the right one, I regret the pain that came with it. I had to live with the constant reminders of guilt. My children were only six and three years old at this time. Their unconditional love, innocence and confidence in me as their mother was the one thing that kept me in a place of strength. At the time of my divorce, I was working on a masters degree in international business, running my fitness company, had one foot out of the door in corporate America, and was taking care of my kids full time.

Today, when looking back, I realized nature knew exactly why something had to come off of my plate. I had the external appearance of a lion, but for anyone who was close enough to me and really paying attention, I was as weak and fragile as a lamb. I made a very comfortable place for cancer to nest in; I was emotionally broken, financially broken, spiritually broken, and living on what was physically left of me, draining my body to keep things going.

# "I Was Emotionally Broken, Financially Broken, Spiritually Broken, and Living On What Was Physically Left Of Me."

The final decisions of this legal struggle were delivered to me by an attorney who I believed was wrong for me in many ways. I chose a woman who happened to be white, was very well-off and did not have strong ties within the city of Atlanta, but her fair share of struggle gave her enough empathy to fight the right way for me as my legal representative. When it was announced to me that the child custody decision put my children with their dad for majority of the year although we had joint custody, I could not breathe.

At that point, I felt like I no longer possessed what my children had given to me to keep me going, and I became lost and swallowed by fear. I felt my life was over, and I did not want to breathe. Have you ever felt like you could not breathe? The feeling that the world is closing in on you and everywhere you turn you are facing a brick wall? This part of my life, among many other situations that you will read more about, is the reason why I know you.

I understand how you may be feeling right now in this moment. Listen to my words and read them carefully: YOU CAN MAKE IT THROUGH THIS. Right now, you are being shaped and molded; you are being forced to look at yourself, the real you, in order to determine what parts of you need to go and what parts of you should stay. It is like taking a plant that looks like it should be thrown away when in reality you can save the plant by sloughing what is no longer viable and helping it live and thrive with what is left. That is exactly what God is doing in your life.

You have major purpose, just like every living and breathing thing moving around in this Universe, and with purpose, that means you must not believe that your life is no longer worth anything. You must simply turn around and face yourself, even if you have no answers right now, just stand: you just accomplished the hardest part.

My mother was my saving grace. She was the angel that came to my apartment every day or called me and threatened to come if I did not call her back. When I wanted to bury my head, she would show up and pull it back out. She is not a woman who wants or asks for big things, but she is a woman of great strength and love, and that was exactly what I needed in my life. I don't know where I would be without my mother. I thought when I was lacking when I was younger because I did not grow up with money, but I realize as a grown woman and mother that love is the greatest gift out of everything.

I had a rich childhood and today I fully understand that. It took me some time to swallow without the feeling of a huge knot in my throat and I had to adjust to a new routine as a divorced parent. Although I knew that I wanted to wake up again to see another day, I was still suffering on the inside and wading in the unfamiliar territory of interacting with a man who was still very angry with me. I had to figure out how to do it for the sake of our children. I love my children, which meant I had to figure out a way to walk through that fear.

Remember what F.E.A.R really means: fostering experiences as reality. I had to train my mind how to release the movie that was playing over and over again in my head of the experience inside that courtroom, listening to the false picture that was being painted about my character. I was crying on the inside, and I wanted so badly to run and hide instead of sticking around to face one more day of those awful experiences. I asked God to help me find my way out of the mess that I felt so entangled in. How did I become exactly what I did not want to be: financially unstable, emotionally broken, and a high statistic for black families - a divorced, single black woman.

When you find you are at your bottom, or at least at a place where you are willing to do things differently in order to create change, there is no where to go but up. You will know when you hit it because there will be a strength that begins to stir within you. You may pick up a book that has been staring at you but that you have been ignoring for months. You may get a phone call from someone who delivers words that hit directly home for you, although that may not have been the caller's intention.

For me, it was going to the bookstore and connecting with a book, "The Secret To Letting Go" by Guy Finley. When I read that book, it was the first time I realized how much I was actually looking outward for the causes of my problems. I was blaming every external factor for my situation, including the emotions of what I thought at the time was anger. "The Secret of Letting Go" taught me how to begin looking at myself and asking the question, "What part am I playing in all of this?" Have you ever asked yourself this question while holding yourself accountable and regretting what you may discover?

The moment you begin taking a closer look at the person you are and accepting responsibility for your life, you are on the path to climbing upward. Divorce is a very difficult experience multiplied times thirty when children are involved, but just like anything else with hard consequences, there is an opportunity to overcome and grow; it just depends on when you decide you are ready.

Are you ready to move upward or will you stay in place and spin your wheels while fostering experiences as your reality?

## CANCER

Following my divorce, my life had completely changed. I went from living in a beautiful home in South West Atlanta to a two bedroom apartment in the city. Life had taken a new path, and I needed to begin figuring things out. I was pursuing a full-time fitness career in personal training and had finished the M.B.A. program at Mercer University; the number one question for myself was what I had to do at that point in time to survive and make enough money.

I can look back now and admit I had no clue; I was just living day by day. I was still in pain from the events that took place during the divorce, and I could not find peace within myself from it all. The irreconcilable feelings were destroying my confidence as an entrepreneur, a mother and a woman. The stress that I carried day in and day out finally caught up to me on the day I felt a small pea-sized knot embedded within the skin on the left side of my chest.

# "My Whole Life Ran Through My Mind in a Flash"

My whole life ran through my mind in a flash all the way to my funeral. I could not believe the overwhelming feeling the day cancer announced its presence in my life. I am sure I am not the only person who can relate to this feeling when sickness presents itself. I say PRESENT because disease does not just happen out of nowhere; it is a disruption that begins well in advance from obvious signs.

Stressful situations that hang around longer than they should is when your health becomes at risk. Stress triggers D.I.R.E situations, which means it will disrupt proper function of your digestive, immune, reproductive, and excretory system. This is also known as dysbiosis, a microbial imbalance in the body. I did not want to know what was going on when I found this knot; I could only think about the fact that I did not have any money to see a doctor and, therefore, that was going to be my excuse.

However, subconsciously I did want to know, because I shared what I found with a friend, who encouraged me to go to the doctor and offered to help by paying for the visit. Now I was all out of excuses. That visit to Piedmont was a challenge for me. I was scared of the unknown, I was scared of a system that I did not fully embrace, and I was more afraid of moving further away from the time I needed to get back with my children. They needed me, and here I was now layered with another possible problem.

I left the doctor's visit with very few definitive answers and a recommendation to have a biopsy. I hated the experience of being lured down a dark rabbit hole and having a lack of control. Compared to everything else that I did not have control over in my life, I always felt like I could rely on my body responding exactly the way that I wanted it to through diet and exercise.

Everything I believed in was now up for question. Was my whole belief system a lie? If not, why am I possibly facing such a harsh disease. Everyone I recall battling cancer around me lost the fight. I was afraid of transitioning without accomplishing anything that would benefit others, including my children. I was so disappointed in myself because to me, my life looked like a complete failure, and now I had a serious disease. When I arrived at my appointment to have a biopsy, I had the thought of jumping in my car at every moment, but I knew I could not stick my head in the sand; I had to find out what was going on with my body.

I met with a female doctor who took one look at the pea-sized bump and assured me without giving me a biopsy that this was just a cyst and I should not be worried. Now, my first grown-up response should have been to do the biopsy anyway, but given the fact that I was looking for a way out, she gave me one without the guilt, and I made my exit from that office as quickly as I could even though the hairs were still standing up on the back of my neck. Something was still wrong; why was that object there if it wasn't cancer? I knew I needed to turn back around, but fear took me to my car because I did not want another problem in my life. I did not want to deal with anymore stress as I was already buried in it. F.E.A.R is not real; it is how we foster our past experiences and use them as excuses when we don't want to face something in our life.

I made a very bad mistake because of F.E.A.R; a decision to keep walking and ignore my health. When you begin trying to shut out the voice that is more powerful than your human self, I encourage you to turn around and listen. Listen to it when it is tapping you on your shoulder and telling you not to run. I have no regrets now, but if I had to do it all over again, the story would have played out with me staying at the office and having that biopsy. Before I knew it, two years rolled by, and my little bump was now an obvious bump that I could no longer ignore.

From the size that it had taken on and the fact that it was growing, it could no longer be mistaken for a cyst. I remember the day my daughter saw my chest and asked me what it was. She then asked me when I was going to go to the doctor. My partner followed her some days later, telling me he was concerned. I was receiving the message loud and clear; it was time for me to stop running. In January of 2011, I was officially given the news that I had a malignant tumor in the left side of my breast. It was in that moment that I started thinking about all of the things I really enjoyed doing and if those activities would be interrupted.

The conversation about chemotherapy and what it would do to my body and how I would feel became a muffled sound to me. I was not ready to walk that path and I did not feel like it was what I was supposed to be doing. Learning to listen to yourself in spite of the words that others may feed you is important. There may be an important decision that you need to make right now in your life, maybe about your health, or your money; learning to trust yourself is the most important because there is always more than one right answer.

If your only answer for problems that require important decisions are only being fed by the fears of others, you will only experience fear-based consequences. In other words, nothing good will come from making decisions that are not made from a place of truth and love. I made the decision to decline undergoing chemo when medical professionals recommended I take that path. I had to go home and face all of the other elements that were driving the birth and survival of this disease; chemo would have been one more disruption in my life that would have dragged me further away from truth.

# "Nothing Good Will Come From Making Decisions That Are Not Made From A Place Of Truth And Love."

<u>Spiritual Awakening</u>

Like many of us, throughout my childhood I was handed my beliefs through a non-denominational Christian religion. The difference between rights and wrongs were emphasized over and over again in the church and in my home. I was told that tithing would bless my life with wonderful gifts. I heard miraculous stories from others about the miracles and blessings they received because of tithing. I was told I must pray to God and ask for what I want in order for me to receive it.

I was given the steps necessary for becoming a good Christian, and I indoctrinated those beliefs throughout my adult life until the day I began raising questions. This was the day I came home knowing I had cancer and that I had a fight on my hands. I had to begin digging into my life in order to learn who I really was and what contributions I was supposed to make during the years I have to left in this human form.

I didn't know those answers. Hell! I didn't know a whole lot at that point, and I was willing to begin admitting that because here I was experiencing another rock bottom. I thought the change that occurred from going through a divorce and losing time with my children was my bottom, but now cancer? I was afraid of leaving my life without leaving an impactful footprint for my kids so they could dodge the mistakes I made about relationships, money, religious beliefs, and other parts of my journey. My whole world that I thought existed had now been turned upside down.

A medical doctor who taught patients about Qigong meditation visited me. I learned how to breathe, allowing positive energy into my body and releasing toxic energy out. I felt a little weird on days we sat silently together breathing over the phone, but I had nowhere else to go and I knew I needed some help. He introduced me to a book called "The Infinite Way" by Joel Goldsmith, a man I have grown to respect and appreciate. His book was the turning stone in my life, and I found much comfort in all of the new teachings I absorbed as a spiritual connection rather than a religious belief.

For me, that book stripped away the things that really didn't matter and helped me to put my focus on spiritual understanding. It was then I began realize to that everything in my life that I was judging myself so harshly about was not even important. The real importance all came down to love and spiritual consciousness. Everything we do in life should come from a place of love, and when it does not, it is not that it defines us as bad people, it just provides crucial information about our spiritual awareness.

Some of us operate on higher spiritual planes than others. This is not because one is better over another, it just means that karmic law forces evolution to happen at different times in life for different people. Through the teachings of others, by way of meditation and reading, I was able to begin forgiving myself for various things in my life that I had been holding onto.

This experience was only the beginning of my journey to natural healing. There is more yet to share with you, but just like all change, it only comes when you make the first step towards something different. In order to become different, think differently and attract different things into your life, you must be willing to work on changing the magnetic flow that has been gathering inside of you since you first began having experiences as a child.

Maybe you saw your family struggle and are, like I was once, afraid deep down that there will never be enough. Maybe you always had more than others, and while trying to fit in with your peers, you became ashamed of having more or being more. Maybe you were around plentiful resources, but those in charge held onto everything out of fear of losing it all. There are so many challenges people face on so many different levels that without learning how to sit still and change the vibrational flow, you will always continue to attract the circumstances that you run from.

Spiritual realignment is learning how to understand the power you possess inside of yourself, meditating in order to turn it loose, and trusting the process. I want you to take a moment right now and write down what you need more of and what you want to remove from your life. Now, on the other side of that paper, write down what you need to do in order to begin moving in that direction. Repeat what you intend to accomplish everyday and what you need to do in order to execute these changes.

Also, at the very beginning and end of this exercise, I want you to write down what you deserve. I wake up every day saying out loud, "I deserve to be wealthy, there is more than enough, I am healthy and I am whole." I had to become those words in order to remove all negative thoughts fighting for room inside of my mind. I had to consciously put everything that I wanted different in my life into action, and you must do the exact same thing.

This formula is not something new; you have either heard it all before and did not trust it enough to do it, or you just weren't ready to embrace the work that is required to change the course of your life. You must be ready to do the work. I read in a book by Les Brown called "The Laws of Success" that "how you do anything is how you do everything." I could no longer accept mediocrity if I want to become great.

# "I Could No Longer Accept Mediocrity If I Want to Become Great."

The bottom line is, you must be willing to leave all old aspects of your life behind if they are not serving you and your life well. Even if that means raising relevant questions about the religious rules you were taught to follow or evaluating the real value of the relationship you are in currently. Be willing to face the truth in exchange for what you really want in your life. It is the only way you can begin to experience something different. I had to do it, and every successful person who is not only making money but also filled with peace, love, happiness and joy had to go through it as well. The choice is up to you.

I have taken you on a brief journey through all of the necessary topics for you to gain a better understanding and move forward in your learning. I shared with you my three biggest challenges in life: money, health, and divorce.

I also shared with you a few short stories about what I had to overcome to experience something different because it is important for you to know that no matter what you are facing in your life, you are not facing those problems alone. People all over the world are struggling to overcome health problems, a bad divorce, money issues, and loss. The world is filled with challenges and, no matter how bad things may feel, I was motivated to gather enough courage and write this book to be one if not the first, people to show you that you can OVERCOME all things.

Before we move forward, put a mirror in front of your face and tell yourself "I can overcome all things." Every day you wake up and start to feel anxiety setting in; when you are apprehensive about investing the last little bit of money you have been saving but you know it is a smart decision, remind yourself that you are overcoming all things. I will share with you the steps you must take to get past some of the obstacles in the areas of your life that are causing you to stay stuck.

When I was in my thirties and felt so lost but hungry for some direction, I wish I had found someone who could not only inspire me to want to do better but show me what steps I could take to begin moving in that direction. I work with a small group of young girls and women who are thirsty for something better in life but don't necessarily have someone speaking the right words to them to help them get on track and avoid getting lost in the world. The world will suck you in and swallow you if you aren't paying attention.

## "Television, music, bad crowds of people, and family are part of the world and there is always some negative influence within each of these groups."

Television, music, bad crowds of people, and family are part of the world and there is always some negative influence within each of these groups. When you decide it is time to abandon the habits and people that are not helping you move forward, you are ready to move; the next important part is know-how. No one gets a pass on challenges; they help us grow and force us to learn more about ourselves in order to put us on the path of purpose.

I believe that money and health are the top areas of challenge that trickle over into other segments of our lives, potentially creating other problems. We will spend most of our time together talking about money and health because money is a topic most never want to talk about but want more of, and health is also a very private area. Many secretly have more health issues than they are willing to admit. I believe it is important to talk about anything that is important enough to destroy or build our quality of life.

# 4 E.A.T. - LETTING GO

EAT stands for Emotional Alkalinity Therapy and in in four easy steps, I will show you how to apply EAT in your life in order to begin letting go of the emotional baggage caused by psychological misfortunes.

These four steps will not only open the space for peace of mind, they will also invite forgiveness and open your mind to the realization that there is nothing to be afraid of and that there is no need to force anything you want in this world.

## 1) Acknowledging Judgment

Whenever you are critical of yourself and others, it's usually because you have unresolved issues with yourself.

After my divorce, I was angry about my financial hardship. I worried about struggling to pay my mortgage. I often wondered how I was going to make it from week to week.

I remember hating Mondays because I knew that my phone would ring constantly with calls from bill collectors.

My email inbox would be full of messages from my attorney, who in hindsight was getting paid to create more mess and additional stress in my life in order to pad the invoices.

The main realization that I had to come to acknowledge and understand about myself was that self-judgment had nothing to do with my expectations for myself. Rather, it was my judgment of my parents. As a child, I only focused on seeing the hardship and struggle. I hated being told, "No, we can't afford it." At an early age, I decided that I never wanted to feel that way.

Hence, my disappointment in myself was highlighted because now I was at a point in my life when I should have been in control, but instead I was right back to feeling the same way I did as a child.

I judged my parents when in actuality I should have been thanking them. After all, they gave me something so invaluable in life: love and the encouragement to do better.

They did the best they could, but initially, I did not want to see it that way. I needed someone to blame. How are you judging your circumstances today? Are you seeing your current situation through your childhood eyes? How are you judging the parties who were involved in those experiences and who are you blaming?

Take a moment to walk through your mind with honesty, identifying what you felt as a child and how those feelings factored into the development of your coping mechanisms and do this exercise when you are able to take 20-30 minutes of undivided time.

Write the following:
1. The names of all parties involved in your influence
2. What you felt in the experiences with them
3. What you decided for your life as an adult as a result of those experiences

Now that you have identified the root of your emotions, let us move forward.

_____

_____

_____

_____

_____

_____

_____

_____

_____

_____

_____

_____

_____

_____

_____

_____

_____

_____

_____

_____

_____

_____

_____

_____

## 2) **Recognizing God's hand**

Fear is the natural, emotional, and instinctive response to a perceived or imaginary threat. Its purpose is to serve as a warning signal in the face of danger and instability. We're prompted to either face it or avoid it.

Comparatively, our mental experience of fear becomes an issue because it can be initiated by our imagination rather than actual events. Two years after going through a difficult divorce, reestablishing myself a single woman with children, and being diagnosed with breast cancer, I often wondered, what now? I woke up most mornings concerned about whether my life could possibly end prematurely. I worried that I may miss seeing my children grow into adults and having families of their own.

I began associating everything with mortality, which only left me feeling paralyzed in my own mind. I felt that I was being punished. I questioned myself for choosing to divorce.

I regretted that my children were now spending more time with their father than with me. I wondered whether maybe I had been too selfish and not generous enough. I was lost, angry, and wanted to give up. I felt like I had the right to give up on God since I felt as though he had given up on me. But in every moment I tried to let go, an unexplainable experience would happen to me.

Different people (whom I call angels) who I never actually laid eyes on entered my life for brief moments, leaving me with the strength I needed to begin rising up and recognizing that what I had to face was beyond just me, and that I was chosen as the object of a bigger purpose. I then began to understand that it was time for me to surrender myself to a process that was beyond me.

I was reminded that God never left me; I had just stopped listening to him. When your health is compromised, you will find that people will challenge you and that relationships will become troubled. Yes, God allows things to happen, but only for one of three reasons: to teach, to learn, or to reveal a bigger purpose. I encourage you to view your challenging experiences as ones of value.

Our challenges present us with opportunities to understand more about ourselves. How many different challenging circumstances can you look back on and recognize that you helped to teach someone else, or that you learned something about yourself, or that it helped put things in perspective in order for you to let things go?

Had it not been for the experiences in my life that I felt I was being punished for, you would not be reading these words from me today. God is always present, regardless of what you're going through. The moment you stop fighting against a force that is necessary and make a conscious decision to embrace it as truth, you can then look forward to healing, teaching, and allowing something greater to happen in your life. You can then pass your strength to others as I am now passing this on to you.

## 3) **Forgiving and surrendering the emotion**

In this third step, we must identify the true emotion tied to the disease and then learn how to release it back into the universe by rerouting our subconscious thoughts. Many patients come to me to achieve "emotional alkalinity."

They come to me thinking that they are sad, only to discover that they are actually lonely.

It is important to recognize the correct emotion associated with an experience. Identifying the emotion is the only way the journey to true healing can begin. I never felt like I was truly angry at my former husband for what he did to challenge my character as a mother, but it was the only word that came to mind. I later learned that I was using unnecessary energy and attempting to conquer the wrong emotion.

Resentment and guilt were actually the two emotions that plagued me. These are also two emotions commonly associated with an individual's fight against cancer. I must emphasize the significance in understanding how harmful it is to harbor guilt and resentment. In her book "You Can Heal Your Life," author Louise Hayes identifies every disease with the true emotion that correlates with it, and lends a powerful affirmation to begin reprogramming the subconscious mind.

## 4) Embracing the Opportunity

It's time to look at your seemingly negative experiences with a positive eye. Sift through your mind carefully and recall the moments when you were able to smile during a hurtful experience. What positive things do you remember about the people who brought you the most pain? What purposeful moments might not have occurred without that painful experience? What funny things happened during those times?

The subconscious mind has a tendency to put bad things on the surface and bury happy moments; therefore, we must consciously pull those happy moments out in order to begin eliminating the negative energy. Within one week of being told I had a malignant tumor, I went from depression and fear to being hopeful and excited. I chose to deal with my true emotions.

I chose to receive the path I had been given to walk, and to see my plight as something with a larger purpose. I accepted my role in that bigger purpose and chose to look forward to the opportunity of touching the lives of others in their journey towards healing. In the beginning, I, much like you, did not know where to turn for help, but my desire to understand and to heal brought that help into my life. I did not want to allow my fight against breast cancer to become what it is for many: emotional defeat.

I made a conscious decision to associate my struggle with joy and triumph. This report may be the beginning, middle or end of healing for you. Regardless of where you stand in your journey, I encourage you to view your past with strength and confidence and know that without pain, there is no real pleasure. I encourage you to continue your path on "emotional alkalinity."

It saved my life and keeps me in alignment with my true self today. I still experience life challenges; the difference is that when they appear I have no worries, stress or anxiety because I only see my glass as half full and not half empty. Your experiences are dictated by your beliefs. It only takes a small ounce of faith to move yourself beyond difficult moments. Now that we have addressed one of the most important steps, which is letting go and embracing your fears, you are on your way and ready to move to the next step. It is important to note, however, that this step will be ongoing for you if you were able to go through the exercise and if you are willing to put in the work to experience a new direction.

## Assessing The Damage

When stress is ongoing in our lives, we really have no idea of the extent of the damage. We have to live life daily, which means that if we don't try and keep up with it all, we fall behind. Falling behind can only add more anxiety to it all. For women, it's even more complex because if children are included, it is keeping up and managing each individual life for them. For example, if you spend many years eating out and not exercising, you may look up one day after all of the damage has been done carrying 50 pounds more than you did two years ago. Why didn't you notice it when it was happening? It is too difficult to see everything that is going on in real time. We don't see a clear picture of our reality until we have a moment to look back.

In this case, because you are in repair mode and embracing truth in your life; you are taking a moment now to look back and acknowledge what damage has taken place. This is, in my opinion, one of the second hardest things to do because you are not only looking out the door to see what happened while your blinders were on, you are really opening the door and allowing emotions to also flow inside.

This may cause you some pain, anger, sadness, guilt, and resentment that you thought you took care of in the past. The truth is, toxic emotions that are not addressed in a healthy way only wreak havoc when shelved and tucked away. These emotions only become toxic because they are treated with disrespect. This is the tornado of damage that must be evaluated, and relevant areas of your life must be considered.

# 5 YOUR HEALTH

I briefly touched on the importance of spending time focusing on your health. When we are born, most of us all have the opportunity to operate from a place where there is physical activity, running, jumping, and playing as a child. The tone for your relationship with food is established through the habits of your family when you're young. If mom made sure bread came with every meal, that is what you became accustomed to and will likely do as an adult. If grandma prepared a warm bowl of grits for you with sugar, cream cheese and butter, you become emotionally attached to the taste, smell, and the experience of love associated with that dish.

Food relations develop in our early years, which change the course of your life from birth. The problem with food habits that are passed on are that they can ignite the beginning of ongoing health challenges and become disruptive in your pursuit of happiness. It is not only food habits that are passed on, there are also habits established as young adults, possibly due to financial limitations or social pressures.

The point that I am making with this information is that without being healthy, your dreams and aspirations of success are limited. You can set yourself on a path of making lots of money and building a great future, although the question becomes: when you have made lots of money, do you want to have to spend it all on medical bills from creating a revolving door for doctor visits? Do you want to take money and invest it in healthy food and assurance of regular exercise or would you prefer to invest it in a medical practice and hospitals? These are very important questions that you must be willing to answer.

I associate health and wealth together because they go hand in hand once you decide you want full control of your life. I remember laying on my couch following the completion of chemo, asking myself what more I needed to do to continue growing, and I found myself enrolling back into school to study neuroscience. I wanted to learn and understand more about the circuitry in the brain.

What I have always understood is that exercise releases feel-good chemicals in the brain, but from a morphological explanation, it's a little more complex. When you exercise, movement creates excitation sending signals through neuronal activation, which transmits signals to the brain and releases a natural dopamine that makes you feel good and gives you the mind power to accomplish anything.

What many people don't realize is that food has the same process except proper nourishment passes through the blood-brain barrier and feeds the regions that control fear and emotions and help with cognitive function, vision, and more.

There are so many important reasons why the practice of good health is beneficial; a whole book could be dedicated to this topic alone. But for the purposes of this journey, I will stick to how becoming healthy and maintaining that health all ties into you making one of the most important decisions of your life. You are important, and you must begin to change your subconscious mind from putting yourself last to moving your needs first.

When I realized I had to battle breast cancer, I felt betrayed by my body. I had only looked at my life from a very narrow point of view. I invested everything in me to carry an external picture of health, when in fact, I was not on the inside. Yes, for the most part I ate vegetables everyday and applied the discipline to stay away from processed foods, sodas, and going overboard with sugar, but I was lacking a fundamental principle.I was not eating for life, I was eating for looks.

## "I was eating for looks, not for life"

<u>Eat For Life</u>

Advertisements, social media, television, they all send subliminal messages that influence the way we think, how we feel about certain issues of the world, and how we begin to feel and see ourselves. There are multiple conversations on eating healthy to look healthy, but not much emphasis is put on eating healthy to be healthy.

People are willing to do whatever it takes to obtain the look, but in the process of reaching the overall objective, your health could be jeopardized.

As a young college student, I was drawn to muscle and fitness magazines. I loved the women who had female gladiator physiques. There was something about that strength that was sexy and appealing to me. This was during a time when the appearance of muscles on a woman was not fully accepted and if you had them, you were thought of as being gay. I didn't care; I was on a quest to obtain that look, and I didn't really understand anything about what was really safe as long as it was legal. I put my mind and energy into working out and it gave me confidence, a energetic release that made me feel in control, and a look that was turning heads wherever I went.

After my first child, I had the new challenge of how to get my body back, and this time I had to pay closer attention to the food. I recall going to the gym and looking at a few of the other women who had it together, thinking that was where I needed to be. I was introduced to a fat burner that had an ingredient in it called Effedrin; the next best thing to a cup of caffeinated coffee at the time. It not only woke you up and surged you with a shot of energy, it sped up your metabolism, creating faster weight loss.

Eventually, the FDA came in and mandated that Effedrin be removed from all products. It was deemed an illegal substance, but by this time I was a fat burner addict and could not get through a workout properly without a pill. I was addicted to the way a fat burner helped keep my body looking and was addicted to the way it made me feel while working out. I barely had any energy and could hardly make it through a full workout without it.

At this point, I had exhausted my adrenals and was a on a path of dysbiosis, which is a disruption in physiological balance. I did not know what I had done, all I was certain of was that I had to keep going and did not have the time to take another path for the sake of my health. I know that this story speaks to many; I am not the only person who was willing to do whatever it took in order to maintain a certain body image that was not only acceptable to myself but to the world. Your health is the one priceless asset that you have that cannot be traded in.

Your body is a magnificent structure created by a power and force that will never be fully understood by science. Man will study the human body until the end of time and the answers will only lead to more questions. As much as your body can be kind, it can be unkind for you. When it is abused, the response is always a great price to pay. When and what that price is, one never knows. If you want greatness in your life, you must be willing to look at your health and give it the same respect and time you give anything else in life.

Think of your health like an investment and set aside a little bit of time daily to do something good for your health. Exercise with care, eat consciously until you learn how to eat healthy without it being something you have to think about, and visualize walking through your life and living your dream as a healthy individual.

**"Think of your health like an investment and set aside a little bit of time daily to do something good for your health."**

American agricultural influencers tell the American people to eat lots of meat for protein, drink milk for strong bones, and take in carbohydrates in the form of starch for energy. Because we have followed this advice, we are not in a good place when it comes to our health. There are a higher rate of millennials who are being diagnosed with cancers, having strokes, and spending money and resources to combat all types of physical and mental issues.

It would be a crime if we continue to pretend that the progressive changes in our food system have nothing to do with this trend. If our country's leaders turn a deaf ear, you must decide not to follow. Your present and future depend on you taking care of yourself by controlling your diet and your health as much as possible. You can plan a great future for you and your family, but the money you make will only carry you so far. No amount of money in the world can buy you another liver or another heart, and no amount of money can buy you out of the battle against cancer. No amount of money can buy you a pass against the consequences from ignoring your responsibility for your health.

My intent is not to beat you over the head about the importance of health, but we don't spend enough time making a plan for our future health while we simultaneously make plans for future earnings. If you want to enjoy your labor of love over the years, I encourage you to begin creating a plan to be healthy.

## Health Plan

So, how do you go about creating a health plan? Well, here is what you will need to first begin thinking about. How you want to feel in the next 10 years and what activity you want to continue doing for those 10 years. Some may say they want to continue working out and playing tennis while another may want to be able to ride a bike and go hiking. One might want to continue running marathons and competing in triathlons. How you feel and what you do to continue feeling that way is the plan that must be created. For example, I have a client who is fifty-six years old, she told me that ten years ago, she wanted to be able to continue moving with fluidity and continue weight training and running. Together, we created a plan that included the primary foods she needed on a regular basis as well as those that she developed an allergic reaction to over the years that she needed to avoid. Regardless of her hectic schedule, she committed to the regular exercise for physical and mental strength.

Some weeks were not so great, but her overall average was great because there were other weeks she was able to play catch up and put in extra work. My point in sharing this woman's story is to show you that life will always happen, and if you sit around taking no action, there will be no positive return connected with the Universe to provide you the things you so desire.

Now that you have decided how you want to feel over the next 10 years and what you want your body to continue doing, you must write these things down in a journal; it can be a journal that is used solely for your health journey or that you use for creating all of the plans in your life. Keep this journal wherever you are when you become the most creative in your imagination.

Next, begin writing under each goal what it will take in order for you to achieve these things. If you want to feel like you did when you were thirty-five or just overall youthful, you must begin looking at the foods that are alive and full of energy. This means that you must begin minimizing the amount of dead foods (cooked and processed) in your diet in order to begin looking and feeling the way you eat. This step is never an easy process, but if you respect the fact that it is a process and try not to decide for yourself how long changing habits is supposed to take, you have a fighting chance to get exactly what you intend to obtain.

Learn to begin reading about food, where it comes from, how is it preserved, and if it originates from another country. Find out if most of what you are eating is genetically engineered and begin understanding how those things could possibly impact your health goals. I would encourage you to read articles on the Internet with caution. If news media delivers information with hidden intentions, Internet media is not much different. Pay attention to the source of information. If you do not know the source well enough to have confidence in the information, double and triple check the information for accuracy. Begin looking at your health the way you may look at the care for an animal, a child or a plant; it requires a little bit of attention daily.

They say it takes twenty-one days to change a habit, but I had to change many habits, and there is a whole lot more to it than that. If anything, it takes twenty-one days to determine how bad of a habit you have and the amount of work it will require to begin making those changes. Think about it; if you have been eating unhealthy, eating something sweet after every meal or eating bread with every meal for at least 3 years, how is it you can expect to change that habit you have adopted in just twenty-one days? That is like a heroin addict or alcoholic going into a twenty-one day drug rehabilitation program and then coming out with the idea that life as an addict is behind them. Eating patterns become an addiction and just like trying to get off of drugs, sobering up is just the beginning. Remember, if you think like an investor with your health as an investment, you will be reminded that it will take a little bit of work at a time, and eventually you can achieve the overall objective.

So you decided you want to clean up your health and you need to understand where to start. You begin the same place as an addict would begin, detoxing mentally and physically. I recommend if you are serious about this change and laying a new foundation, to seek the guidance from a professional wellness expert or, if you don't choose to spend the money, begin reading books about detoxification and what it really means. Many people have been brainwashed to believe that a thorough detox can occur in three days.

Detoxification, by definition, is the metabolic process by which the toxic qualities of a poison or toxin are reduced by the body. It typically takes at least two to three days for toxins to reveal themselves in order for them to begin finding their way into the bloodstream, and that is merely the first layer of toxins. My point here is to emphasize the importance in this first step and relay the time that you may need to properly detox. The reality is that a thorough detox, if you are not combating a disease, is about sixty days long.

The first three weeks is dedicated towards margin of error. You make mistakes, have set-backs, and you don't feel the best. The next four weeks, you start to feel better and notice all of the subtle differences without the foods you had to eliminate. But within this time period, you may also hit what is known as "the healing crisis" where toxins are now being released from the tissues and causing a physical allergic response.

While this makes you think something is wrong, this phase is very important because now you have shifted into a real detoxification. Finally, the last week is a coast, and you have not only entered into a physical release, but spiritually you begin to want to evaluate other areas in your life. The chemicals that are being released from your brain that affect emotions are happy and motivational feelings. The illusions that directly correlate with eating nutritionally empty foods are now gone and you are ready to see a clear realistic picture.

# 6 THE WORK

Now that you have started to clear a path for physical and mental wellness, it is time to take a closer look at who you really are and whether or not you are walking by purpose and with passion. Are you waking up everyday with excitement about what you will spend most of your day doing? If the answer is yes, you are at least in the right lane, but are you making the kind of money you want from that purpose or are you struggling to live? If your answer is no, then I want to help you figure that part out. It is important for you to connect with whom you are, what makes you move to do something without giving it a whole lot of thought. Whatever that is, that is the place you should begin exploring.

We are all here to do something unique for others. Just like we each have a thumbprint that is different from anyone else on this earth, you are different in what gift you have to give to the world. Many live their lives lost and are unable to touch that gift, but if you find yourself reading and moving towards the influences that help you towards your purpose and passion, you have an opportunity to find out who you are and what you have to give to the world.

There is nothing more rewarding than living life each day by waking up grateful for the work you are doing as opposed to the job you force yourself to do because "it pays the bills." A life without passion and purpose is not a life, it is a way to exist while living a human experience.

You are a creative creature, and what lies in each and every one of us is that gift to create new and develop ideas that contribute to propelling the world forward. Slavery no longer exists from a physical sense because there were people who had a vision for the freedom to make choices for themselves. Women's roles in the labor force and leadership positions has grown more dramatically because there were women before me who believed in their right to contribute to the world beyond just raising a family and being a wife. They saw a vision and believed in it enough to react on making it a reality. Millennials, young adults born after 1980, are on track to be the most educated generation because those who believed and envisioned that education as a key to a better world are instilling that dream into present and future generations. You have purpose, and you owe it to yourself and the world to contribute to progress.

I want you to take out a pen and write down on the lines provided below; or better yet, pull out your journal and write down your major purpose. Begin it with "My major purpose is..." I want you to be very clear and detailed in writing this out because this is what you are sending out into the Universe. If you only write down that your major purpose is to help people, what does that really mean? Pulling off an exit and having enough change to give to someone in need? Or maybe when a friend calls you up and needs to talk to you about her troubles you listen?

_____

_____

_____

How do you want to help others and what do you want to accomplish by giving up your time to help? Taking the time to really put some thought behind what you want to spend your human experience doing on this earth is showing respect for not only yourself, but for Universal law.

After you write down your major purpose, put your major purpose in a few different places that you frequent daily. Before I learned my major purpose from heart, I had mine hung up so I could memorize it and be reminded of it throughout my day. I had it on my mirror, on my refrigerator, and written in my journal. I wrote it out, randomly said it out loud, and whispered in my meditation. I still state my major purpose daily. You create your reality, and if it is created by F.E.A.R (fostering experiences as reality), you will be living a life less desirable; a life filled with fear-based results.

The second step is to decide all of the things you want to obtain that are part of your major purpose. For example, you may want to provide more love and care for the elderly through beauty and wellness services. I used this as an example because I have a dear friend who is a hairstylist. We conversed periodically about our dreams, and this was hers. She wanted to give more love and attention to those who invested something into the world and who were now in a place in life where they were in need of others. Her business as a professional hair stylist allowed her to provide that gift to seniors. Throughout our private talks, I suggested that she write down all of her mini goals for providing love and care to seniors through beauty and wellness services. Taking these mini steps allow you to bring your dreams down from five thousand feet to three thousand, which make your major purpose much more realistic because you are creating a road map. She already had the vision and was moving on the path to making her vision into a reality, and we made a commitment to hold one another accountable.

GOALS YOU INTEND TO OBTAIN

_____

_____

_____

_____

_____

_____

_____

_____

_____

_____

_____

_____

_____

_____

_____

_____

_____

_____

Once you determine what things you intend on achieving in your major purpose, underneath each item write out the action steps necessary to achieve your goals. Do you recognize what pattern I have you creating? It is like peeling an onion; once you identify one layer, you peel that back to get to the next layer.

This exercise is not a "complete in one day" assignment, it will take some time for you to think about. However, once you understand your major purpose and the goals you want to achieve have been nailed down, identifying the action steps is a cake walk. The larger portion of your work will be the consistent execution.

## Change Your Routine

We are all creatures of habit. Everyday you wake up, a vast amount of your day is routine. This repetition creates a rhythmic flow, which is unseen, although if you pay attention, you do it without thought. Do you notice however, that when you do something that is outside of your routine or take on an additional responsibility that you must put some thought into getting it done? Well, this scenario is the perfect example as to what has to happen in order for you to begin doing things that are not a normal part of your routine. If your major purpose and goals are something new and not already a part of your life, creating a new pattern will not happen unless you are giving it energy and thought several times within your day. Change requires conscious mental work.

If you want something different, you will need to think about how you need to move all the time before it becomes natural for you to move that way. This is known as living a conscious lifestyle. You are creating a different rhythmic flow by changing your pattern. In order to invite something different into your life, the conscious work must take place first.

## Move With Intention

When you decide to do things different by walking within your purpose and putting your energy back in alignment with the natural flow of the Universe, you must do it with a happy feeling. When you make a choice to do something different in your life, it must be more than just a decision, you must move with every intent of your existence to get it done. Write out the goal, put the action steps behind it, and move with intention. When we are used to doing things according to a certain pattern, we move without thought because we are certain of the response.

When we create a different response by doing something different, it can become a little scary because it's a new experience, which is why you can get stuck in the same place even when you know it is healthier for you to do something different.

Certain expectations are desired but not guaranteed, and this kind of scenario makes all of us nervous. When you are ready to make decisions with unexpected results but are also following a power that guides you from within, you cannot lose.

The lane for what is considered "middle class" is getting smaller as our world continues to change. Soon there will no longer be a lane for it and there will only be one for poor and rich. When this happens, what lane do you want to land in? Every step you make must have a vision and an action accompanied with it.

There must something that you do every day to contribute to the overall objective: envision it, claim it, and act on it. Outliers are those who operate outside of the crowd; they are willing to do the things that most won't do in order to live the life that others want to have. These are the people who, when making a move, do it with every intention on completing what needs to be accomplished no matter what it takes to get it done.

# "Envision It, Claim It, and Act On It."

## Let Old Relationships Go

I mentioned earlier how we are such creatures of habit. We like to know what we are going to get when we react a certain way, even when it is not good for us. Relationships are a big disruption when they no longer serve a positive purpose in our lives. The emotional tie that can be created between two or more people is a book all by itself because there is an invisible connection that cannot be cut with a simple snip, at least not those that have vested time and emotions. There are some relationships that start out very strong, but a lack of invested emotions from those involved can be broken more easily without significant disruption.

Let's spend time talking about disruptive relationships, the ones that have the ability to take power away from you when you aren't paying the right attention to your life. It is a fact that relationships are everything; with friends, lovers, family, co-workers, children, and neighbors, I could keep going for a while, but everything we do in life has to do with a relationship of some sort, and the health of the relationship can determine if the outcome is for you or against you.

People come into our lives through karmic connections. Needs are fulfilled over a period of time; sometimes within a day, months, or even over a lifetime. And recognizing when that time is up can be very healthy, although in many cases it doesn't happen that easily. When there are emotional ties in our personal relationships, those are the hardest to let go of when it is time. You have exposed a side of yourself within that relationship that the rest of the world has never seen; you have invested time, money, and you have grown to love. Unfortunately, when what you are giving and what you need are no longer equitable enough to keep good balance, the situation becomes unhealthy.

The energy created from the relationship becomes toxic, and instead of the intrinsic motivation that used to come from the connection, there is demotivation, which creates a block in your life where everything you are trying to accomplish is either not moving or getting worse.

How do you fix it? Instead of trying to fix "it," you begin fixing yourself. When personal relationships become toxic, pointing the finger outward is so much easier than pointing it at yourself. As children, many of us witnessed blame from one parent to another instead of them acknowledging his or her mistake in a situation. Television and media give us bad news and always tell us who to blame; politicians place blame on other politicians ninety-nine percent of the time, so why wouldn't it seem the most natural that we do it within our own individual lives?

If you want to grow, you have to choose facing yourself. The only way to determine if a relationship is good for you is by you spending the time to understand what part you are playing in the outcome. You may complain about things being bad, but it could very well be your doing.

Whether it is you causing the problem or not, life may be presenting to you that you need time alone in order to see yourself and mature, or that your maturation is calling for a higher vibration that your relationship is not operating on. When relationships around you begin to crumble during your path of growth, be accepting that what is happening is a natural order, and the need to shed old is part of the process.

You have to be willing to abandon everything that cannot go with you when you enter a growing crisis, including the love life you think you have with a particular individual. Starting over in another romantic relationship or the

thought of ending one can become scary, especially if it is the end of a marriage with children, or one that you have been in for quite a long time. It is a connection good or bad that has become a part of your life, but this is a part of the tie that must be broken to allow you to become a better version of yourself. You must swallow the weight that has been pushing on you and do what is best for your peace of mind. This does not mean for you to create drama and stress by going out of your way from outside; you must go deeper inside yourself and ask the Universe, God, Buddha, however you identify your divine power to remove what must go. Be accepting to change and trust how it is presented in your life. Remember, there may be a fight from the opposing side, which is the energy that wants to keep you stagnant. Stand strong and trust the flow of the Universe.

# 7 GROWING CRISIS

When you have had something major in your life occur long enough that you begin looking at life differently, this is when you have entered into a growing crisis. Health is a perfect example and one that I can speak to very distinctly. For me, I experienced both a healing crisis and a growing crisis. When I chose to heal naturally when I was first diagnosed in January of 2011, and I also ventured into a discovery period about who I really was as a person.

I started raising questions about everything that I was doing in my life and learning how I lacked the right tools for making good decisions. I kept dangerous company in my mind, which was an undisputed explanation as to why I was unable to live life the way I imagined it to be.

During this discovery period, I also gained an understanding about the type of spiritual relationship I was actually thirsty for and left religion in my past where it was meant to be. I did not realize how much I was changing until I discussed life in conversations with others. It was then that the Universe knew I was ready for the responsibilities that accompany leadership; I began a growing crisis. The long challenges I had to endure battling cancer, becoming a woman, and opening myself up to being vulnerable to take back my life propelled me forward and aligned me with wealth, good health, and real happiness.

I was no longer the same person I started out to be when I thought I knew everything. Life humbled me and showed me that, in reality, I knew very little. I had to be willing to become a good student who was willing to listen.

## Learn To Listen

If someone asked you if you are a good listener, you would probably say yes because most of us think that we possess this quality. In fact, it is quite the opposite. Most of us are terrible listeners because instead of listening, we spend more time thinking about ourselves. Even throughout the time you may use to pray, I bet you are telling God or however you identify your higher power what you need, how you need it, and the way it needs to happen.

After you finish that prayer, you go on about your day with an expectation that it will happen just as you asked for it. I know this because I used to think like this and, when working with clients who came to me for weight loss or to solve other health issues, this was the expectation. You can have everything you want in life, but you must be willing to sit still and listen without thinking about yourself. Meditation is the tool for listening, which we will discuss a little later, but the listening is not just through meditation, it is also when you are engaging in conversation with others.

How often are you really listening to the other person's words instead of crafting your comeback line while they are talking? I am sure not very often. There is a selfish side to all of us, and it is not that having this quality is bad, it is simply that adopting the ability to listen creates a healthy balance. Becoming a good listener takes practice.

It requires ongoing conscious effort before it naturally occurs when communicating with others. If you desire the ability to open yourself up to what is really going on in the world around you, it would be advantageous for you to adopt or improve your listening.

Listening to others is not the only relevance for this conversation. How often do you hear what I call inner influence telling you to do something and you ignore it?

How often have you ignored that voice and found yourself regretting that you did not choose to listen and follow it? Every time I ignored my inner influence, I had regrets. This voice is not some random moment, it is your voice of reason. We all have it and it exists as our own internal sounding board. Answers lie within you; your work is to understand that when you hear it, you have to trust it. It is a power that you will learn to embrace and understand over time, but life lessons will continue to be presented until you come to a place when you finally hear the message and understand the lesson you need to take with it.

## Be Happy For Others

How often do you find yourself hearing or reading exciting news happening in someone else's life and your initial response is to compare your life and wonder why that something hasn't happened to you? You allow that type of energy to grow internally, creating a jealous emotion.

We are all unique and entered this world at different times in different ways. You will experience happiness, sadness, challenges, pain, anger, and disgust at different times. If you want to create the right energy in your life, you must learn to be happy for others. Even when you know there is a side of you that wants to compare your life, combat the negative emotion by congratulating others.

## "If you want to create the right energy in your life, you must learn to be happy for others."

Social media today has connected people from all over the world, which has its advantages, but on the other hand, studies show that it has been creating depression and distraction among people who spend time reading what others are doing. There is nothing wrong with taking a look at what the rest of the world is doing, but it is also important that when someone you know stirs up a feeling of envy or jealousy, take the time to release that negative energy by combating it with a compliment.

Light always wins over darkness; therefore, positive will supersede negative. More importantly, try and minimize the amount of time you are spending reading about what others are doing. Make sure you take that time and invest it into what you intend to accomplish as your major purpose. If you do not pay attention to how you spend your time and what you spend it on, you will find that you are setting obstacles in your life and disrupting what you want to attract.

Happiness is a choice; you can choose to be happy or you can choose to focus on the things that you blame for making yourself miserable. The energy you spend on the ladder will only keep you sitting in the same place and prevent you from moving forward. Try and choose happiness every day.

Before I left my corporate position, I did not like the way working for the company made me feel. As an example to help get you thinking in the right direction, here is my major purpose:

**"My major purpose is to help solve mental and physical issues by instilling hope and belief in all**

# mankind through spiritual, mental, and physical wellness remedies"

Everyday in my morning routine, I state my major purpose. It took a few days to craft out the right words, but I focused on what I enjoy doing with my time and what I gravitate towards without thinking. I instill hope and belief in others, and I use different wellness remedies that include inspirational speaking, transformational coaching programs, herbal and nutritional methods, and manual services. I state my major purpose at least two to three times throughout my day because it is important to train my subconscious mind to attract people who want the gifts that I have to offer into my space.

I work to attract opportunities into my life that are in line with why I was put onto this Earth. This keeps me organized in making decisions, because as a Taurus/Gemini sign, I have a tendency to pile my plate up with exciting things even though they have nothing to do with my major purpose.

Time is valuable and it is also another commodity besides our health that cannot be bought, so be very careful about what you do with your time and how you spend it. If you don't pay close attention, you can discover that you have invested your time on someone else's dream and have abandoned your own.

## Being Vulnerable

When life kicks into high gear, things can really become a challenge, such as when a relationship has ended, a company in which you have invested many years has handed you walking papers, or like me, you were diagnosed with a complicated disease. It does not matter what the circumstance may be, all it takes is for something to occur that is hard enough to make you become a different person.

When I had no money, my relationship with my children's father was estranged, I was unsure about my major purpose, and was also unhealthy. That was enough to send me to the loony bin, and although it didn't, it was a major turning point in my life because I had to drop my pride and learn how to trust others by allowing them to see where I really was in my life - broken.

Sharing with others, even a small handful of people, that your life is out of order can be a very humbling experience. You feel completely naked and afraid of the unknown- what will others think of me? But when you step up and decide to take ownership for where you are in your life, whether good or bad, and accept it as an opportunity to change the things that need changing and improve the things that can be done differently, you will learn that there are people facing the same struggles or trying to overcome the same emotional crisis.

The fact is that in this life, we cannot get everything done without needing the help of others. When you are in need of help from others, you have to show up without being too proud to tell the truth. You have to be willing to throw the dice and trust that the Universe is already providing you with what you need, whether it comes from those who know your vulnerability or someone sent in response to your situation.

Vulnerability is an eye-opening experience. Your eyes become open to seeing that even after you share these dark secrets, they were only dark because you were too afraid to put them out in the light, and that once you got the courage, they were only ever dark in your mind, not to everyone else. Once again, F.E.A.R is fostering experiences as reality. The image you have painted in your mind about how your life would be perceived is all and only in your mind. Yes, it is true, people are not always nice and there are those who will talk negatively, but those are the people who are miserable within their own lives, and talking about someone else's drama is like self-medicating on alcohol when trying to drown out problems. If you are willing to be vulnerable, you are ready to change the repetitive magnetic cycle that has invited the impact of your circumstances into your life, but you must be willing to stand up and stand out once you decide you are ready.

Being ready is accepting the idea that people are going to have an opinion no matter what you do or how you decide to live your life. However, their opinions cannot be allowed to define you. Their opinions don't belong to you and although they can matter, they do not have to be in control of who you are. You are a powerful human being with flaws.

When you can show the world the side that we all have within ourselves, you can also experience genuine connections that others can't experience when they cannot be vulnerable. For me, this is not something that comes and stays on its own. No, this is something I have to work at on a regular basis. I have to remind myself that it is okay being flawed, and if honesty exposes my flaws, it is okay because I am still a magnificent human being.

Practice Makes Purpose

Change does not come around overnight, especially when you have been practicing other habits for many years. These habits have been carried throughout your life without much thought after they were adopted into your subconscious being. Therefore, changing them is a fight with your conscious mind. It wants to maintain control over what you have been used to doing and thinking.

If you have a stream of poor relationships and you thought they were doomed at the start, or thought that they were too good to be true and wondered what was really wrong with the other person, your ego will not want to surrender that way of thinking just because you want something different in your life. No, changing your mental attitude about anything in life and attracting different experiences, takes practice, practice, practice. Did I say that loud enough? Let me repeat myself:

## "In order to begin attracting different experiences into your life, you must PRACTICE, PRACTICE. PRACTICE"

Every morning, through your day, and at night, a routine should be developed within your mind in order to remove all negative thoughts. The moment you get excited about doing something different, how often do you tell yourself: it can't be done, it is impossible, there is no time, or that family, money and responsibilities will not allow it? How often do you sabotage your dreams? I bet pretty frequently. Learn how to become a child again by believing that anything is possible, because it is. If you can conceive it, it is possible.

Just look at the magnificent creations that you have witnessed in your lifetime, especially since the birth of technology; so much has changed and intelligence only continues to evolve over time. You are not separate from that intelligence, you are a part of it, and what you do with the time that you are present in your human experience is all up to you. Begin believing in you again by practicing the power of a positive mental attitude.

Meditation has become one of my most reliable tools. I cannot get through my day smoothly without it. Meditation creates an invisible shield over my mind and my body, and it protects me from the negative energy that is part of the air we breathe. You may not be able to see the energy but you can definitely feel it. It is a strong force that can grab hold of anyone the moment there is a weakness. When you begin your day weak and with vulnerable energy, you are an easy target to become a carrier of negative energy. Learn to shield your energy from what may be waiting for you throughout your day. You are not in complete control of circumstances, therefore you must prepare yourself to be in the right mental state of mind in case challenges show up.

Choose this exercise in the morning and at night because the beginning and the end are the most important parts of the day. In the morning is that quiet time before it all starts, and at night is when it all ends, but you can have significant impact on where it all goes from there.

There are powerful events that are manifesting for you while you are sleeping. This is why it is important that you give thanks for what is already done. You must believe that your purpose is moving according to plan, although you cannot see it happening.

## 8 IT'S NEVER OVER NIGHT

People often want to set expectations on success the way they set them on weight loss. As soon as you decide you want to lose weight, you want to know how you can make it happen within the next few days. I know because many of my clients who first came to me with the desire to lose weight always asked the same first question: how much can I lose in two weeks, or if I go hard for thirty days can I drop ten pounds? I have always been amazed at the lack of commitment people are willing to give to their bodies in order to achieve change.

The best way I can remove my judgmental mask is to look at how I was in my life when I wanted to become something. I was impatient and expected for things to start moving for me the moment I came up with a great idea, but life is just not that simple. Time is a required investment when you are creating something that will pay out positive returns over a long period of time. If you want to make a lot of money doing what you love, money is only guaranteed when you take the TIME to master what you are doing. To become a master, it takes trying, falling and getting back up to try, fall, and get back up again.

# "To become a master, it takes trying, falling and getting back up to try, fall, and get back up again."

Have you ever watched a good kung fu movie when someone who wanted to become a master in kung fu had to go into the village, adopt life skills and study the art over many years? Sometimes they show a small child who becomes a man, and sometimes a man who matures into a wise old man. If you pay close attention to the movie, it will show you that time must pass in order for that person to become great at that art. This is no different from what is required for any other thing that gives you power.

The power over your health does not happen in three months or six months, it takes place over time. Building wealth isn't investing in a stock and making a million dollars within a year; it is a common rule that you do not invest unless you have money that does not need to be touched for at least ten years.

When you begin working and you choose a profession, you do not become manager over others or vice president of a department within the same year; you must spend time working and learning in order to master the many skills that are necessary in order to be an effective leader over other people. Time is the operative word, it is what cannot be bought, sped up or forced to move differently. It is the one commodity that you can't get back or give away. Time is valuable and it belongs to no one person. It is an undervalued asset that can give you the best life or take opportunity away.

We take time for granted because we want everything in our own time and it just doesn't work that way. You must be willing to put in the time and prepare for the day that you will get something out of investing that time. Treat anything the way you want everything.

## Falling and Knowing How To Get Back Up

After you have released old baggage in your life and are now moving towards change, it doesn't mean that the world is perfect and all is exactly the way it is supposed to be. No, making changes to old habits is like a drug addict going into rehab for sixty days; the work doesn't begin while you are in, it begins when you come out and you have to face the world without your dependency. This is why recovering drug and alcohol addicts fail a number of times before they manage to secure lasting sobriety: relapse is a normal part of recovery.

When changing old habits, whether from childhood or as an adult, it is natural to relapse back into what you have been familiar with.

## The Desire Must Be Greater

Think back on anything you may have wanted badly as a child. Somehow, you knew you had to get cooperation from your parents in order to get it. Did you sit around thinking about the work it would take? No, I am certain you only focused on it happening. If you want to bring it a little closer to home, think about when you may have wanted to start a family but heard so many stories about how hard it is to raise children and the challenges that you face with different personalities and financial responsibilities.

Did hearing how hard it was stop you from starting a family? No, because you wanted it bad enough to only focus on the "why" as opposed to the "what." That attitude should be the same attitude you carry when approaching your destiny. You have to want it bad enough to ignore the energy that will be required for you to get there. You cannot walk through those challenges without your health being in order, but you can get there without having the money. The start begins with you sacrificing, giving everything it takes if what you want is worth it.

You must be willing to hold onto seeing the end instead of being overwhelmed by how it is supposed to happen for you or when. I remember when I knew I wanted to have children, I was afraid of having something so large in size pass through to enter the outside world. I was also uncertain about parenting; I had never been a parent, how would I know what to do and how would I respond when difficult situations occurred?

I was unsure about the whole experience, but the fact that I wanted children and could see it happening with a clear picture, I still had enough courage to walk through that experience just to obtain the reward. You are more in control of your life when you realize you have power. When you decide to embrace that power by connecting your vision and actions together, you are unstoppable, and you will begin to know without doubt there is nothing too impossible.

**"When you decide to embrace that by connecting your vision and actions together, you are unstoppable, and you will know without a doubt there is nothing too impossible."**

# 9 DON'T GIVE AWAY YOUR POWER

Are you aware how often you give your power away? Do you even realize you do it? When I went through my divorce, I was tortured by things my former husband would do to me just because he was still angry and hurt. Instead of denouncing that energy, I received it. I believe that deep down, I carried a certain amount of guilt for wrecking our home by leaving, and I subconsciously believed that I deserved some form of punishment. I opened myself up to allowing someone else to control my life, which was an open invitation for hard times. I gave control of my life to someone else because of guilt, and it took many years for me to figure that out in order for me to take it back and steer my life in the direction that I wanted to travel. I had to forgive myself, spend time alone, read many books, meditate regularly, and learn who I became through such challenging times. If you want to be in control of your life, you have to spend the time getting to know who you are. Do not focus on who you were when you were a child or on how your family did things. No, you have to look at the types of decisions you are making NOW in your life and analyze why you are making them when they have a detrimental impact of the way you live.

It is most likely that you are giving your power away to whomever chooses to make decisions for you: haters, angry people who don't have your best interest in mind, your boss who is already a miserable person anyway, or even a mate who feels he/she doesn't want you accomplishing more than them to cover up their own inadequacies. Your power is very valuable; it is what you need in order to control your life and move towards greatness. Your power is what is required to change the course of your journey when you realize your ship is moving in the wrong direction. Your power is what you need so you can spend that energy on taking proper care of your health to move through your days being productive and thinking effectively. You are a powerful human being with a purpose. If you want to live out your purpose, you have to be willing to look at your life, make changes where necessary, and take back your power. Only give away energy to people and things that are worth it, not people and things that are only in place to weigh you down and distract you. Take back your power and use it for your benefit and for the benefit of the world.

## "Own Your Power"

<u>Love not Fear</u>

Everything you do in life should come from a place of love. Love is the light that opens your life up to new opportunities; it shows you who you really are as a person and what changes are needed in order to become a better version of yourself.

Love is the energy that creates healthy relationships and invites positive experiences into your life. When you allow your decisions to be led by love, you open your life up to positive results. Circumstances are not placed in your life to torture you or to make your human experience unbearable, they are placed in your life to challenge you to becoming a better, more mature human being and teaching you what life is really all about.

**"Circumstances are not placed in your life to torture you, they are placed in your life to challenge you to becoming a better, more mature human being and teach you what life is really all about."**

Love is the energy force that wins all the time, regardless of how you may look at a situation. I was challenged on many levels throughout the earlier years of being divorced. I did not want to fight a man I still loved, but I also did not want to accept angry behavior and bullying. I felt every time that I did nothing, I was losing. I was so tired and ashamed of what we were facing, I felt that I was losing because I did not respond back with the same fear. I felt that I was losing my place as a mother, I was losing the way those who I once thought were friends looked at me, I even thought I was losing in the eyes of my

131

children when I did not respond back with retaliation. It was quite the contrary: because I did not react with fear and worked to stay in a place of love, today he and I can engage in respectful conversation.

When he calls me on the phone, I can associate positive energy with his number and have nothing but respect for a man who has been actively involved in our children's lives. You see, love helped me to see my situation in a completely different light. There are so many women who are heartbroken and who have heartbroken families due to emotional and financial abandonment from the father. I was fortunate enough to understand that, although he and I did not agree on many things, love had enough power to bring us together in peace and harmony to raise our children with enough balance in their lives to become loving, highly intelligent adults.

Love is what allowed my children to overcome the challenges that stem from divorced families. I could have handled my situation very differently by attacking when I was being attacked, as is often our instinct, but I believed in my heart that the day would come when he and I could laugh together again and smile in passing. The time seemed like forever and almost like that day would never come. Love had been working through this process, but it showed up with a presence and restored peace and harmony back into our relationship. Fear drives fear-based results, but give love and that is what you will receive. If you have a situation going on in your life and you still believe you have something greater to achieve, let go of fear and begin making all decisions from love. It will challenge your emotional intelligence, but when you think about the right thing to do, you will realize that love always trumps fear. Practicing this behavior only allows you to move subconsciously in this space. It allows you to learn how powerful you truly are when you allow love to guide your life.

# 10 RUN WITH IT

I have shared an enormous length of my personal journey with you and willingingly opened up my vulnerabilities to you so that you can be reminded that you are never alone. Your walk may feel lonely because no one can take it for you. Redefining success through your physical and mental health gives you a stronger foundation as you continue on your journey through life. Although I hit on many topics, they are all part of the ingredients needed to move differently and with intention. You are the only person who can decide if you want your life to improve. The tools are not difficult to collect, it is having the strength and motivation to stop using what is not working and doing the things that not only allow you to work smarter but also work less. Everyone has a story; I told you mine because it motivated me to use it as an anchor instead of a shackle. An anchor keeps a ship steady while a shackle confines your mobility.

While everything is changing and moving around you, it is important to have the things in life that will ground you and keep you steady while you are moving through the challenges and experiences that will shape you. Taking care of your body, mind, and spirit makes all the difference in the world when you want to push yourself beyond the mediocrity. It is the difference between a person who can make a lot of money but still have a void and a person who can make a lot of money and maintain happiness. Whatever your desires are in life, they are not impossible to conquer, but the work to obtain them calls for your undivided attention. You may need to leave people and things behind in the process. While you are making necessary changes to do better, don't leave out the importance of taking care of your health. It defines how you think, the kinds of relationships you will have, the energy you attract into your life, and the way you handle experiences. My life was filled with challenges that I never imagined I would have to face. I claimed I would do something big when I was a child, which means I was given what I asked for except I had no input into the process of getting me there.

You may not have a choice in how the Universe plans to give you everything you ask for, and if you are not mentally and physically strong enough for the journey you may not be capable of getting there, and well, let's just say you will understand very quickly why there are very few at the top.

You don't have to know exactly where to begin, just start and the flow of life will do the rest. Work towards practicing everything that we discussed because these are invaluable tools that you will continue to need along the way. Good health and prosperity is your birth rite, and when you begin to claim it and put into motion the actions that pair up with the belief, you will begin to experience something very powerful in your life. You will find that more work is required from within and there is so much love waiting for you. It is yours waiting for you to claim it. Be victorious in your life, redefine the way you look at taking care of your body and understand that it is a way in guaranteeing your ability to be great, no matter what you choose to do in your lifetime. You are here for a reason, you are filled with a purpose. Live life to its fullest, be your best, be healthy first, and remember power is something that already belongs to you, learn how to own it!

# ABOUT THE AUTHOR

Dr. Maria Barnes is a very straightforward, transparent, and bold inspirational speaker, transformational coach, naturopathic doctor, author, and entrepreneur. She has been practicing as a holistic doctor with the belief that true healing is all about bringing into balance body, mind and spirit. Dr. Bee is a woman dedicated to her work, her family, and her friends and believes that when one is ready to make life happen at its highest level, it is then the individual is ready to awaken.

69910485R00082

Made in the USA
Columbia, SC
25 April 2017